Cats of Havana, Cuba

A TRAVEL PHOTO ART BOOK

LAINE CUNNINGHAM

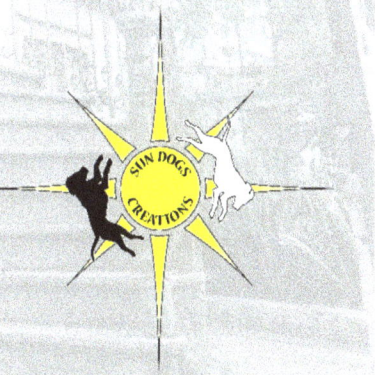

Cats of Havana, Cuba

A Travel Photo Art Book

Published by Sun Dogs Creations
Changing the World One Book at a Time
Print ISBN: 978-1-951389-10-9

Cover Image by Laine Cunningham
Cover Design by Angel Leya

Copyright © 2023 Laine Cunningham

All rights reserved. No part of this book may be reproduced in any form or by any means, electronic, mechanical, digital, photocopying or recording, except for the inclusion in a review, without permission in writing from the publisher.

Havana, Cuba is home to a clowder of cats. The government offers few rescue or care options, so local businesses and individuals set out food. These informal adoptions develop into friendships, complete with stroking and purrs. Restaurant cats and café cats are as likely to greet visitors as church cats. In a country where food scarcity is a daily issue, the compassion and affection shown to these feral residents is special.

Bicolor and tabby cats, ginger and tortoiseshell kittens, calicos and color points prowl the tourist districts and outlying neighborhoods. Juniors wander their territories while those in their prime lounge on steps. During the hottest hours, Havana's cats nap in the shade under palm trees. As the day cools down, they visit the buildings where, after a patient wait, they will be fed. Wander with the cats to see Havana, Cuba from their eyes.

PARADISE

CONTENT

HOMECOMING

SUAVE

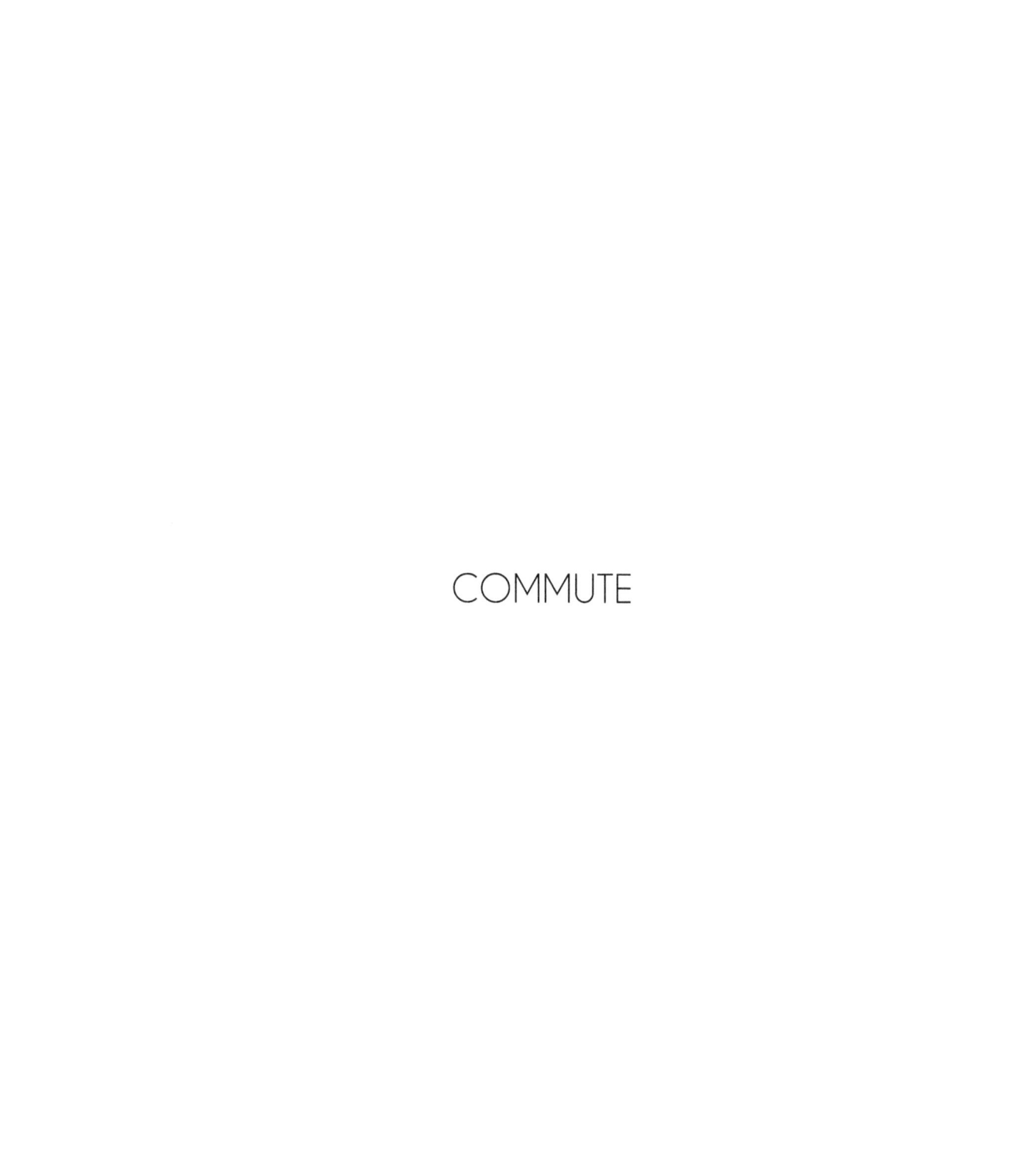

COMFORT

VIGILANCE

HMPH

PROWL

HMM

PRIMED

TRANQUILITY

SEEKER

CURIOSITY

SINGULAR

REGAL

CHILL

WHAT

PATIENCE

ENTHRONED

FOCUS

SIESTA

YUM

BUDDIES

HUSH

STROLL

INTENSITY

KNOCK KNOCK

YO

BUSY

YAWN

GOLDEN

FLUFF

CURVES

FRIENDSHIP

AMBIANCE

SPHYNX

I SEE YOU

PAWS

SIGH

ATTITUDE

SINUOUS

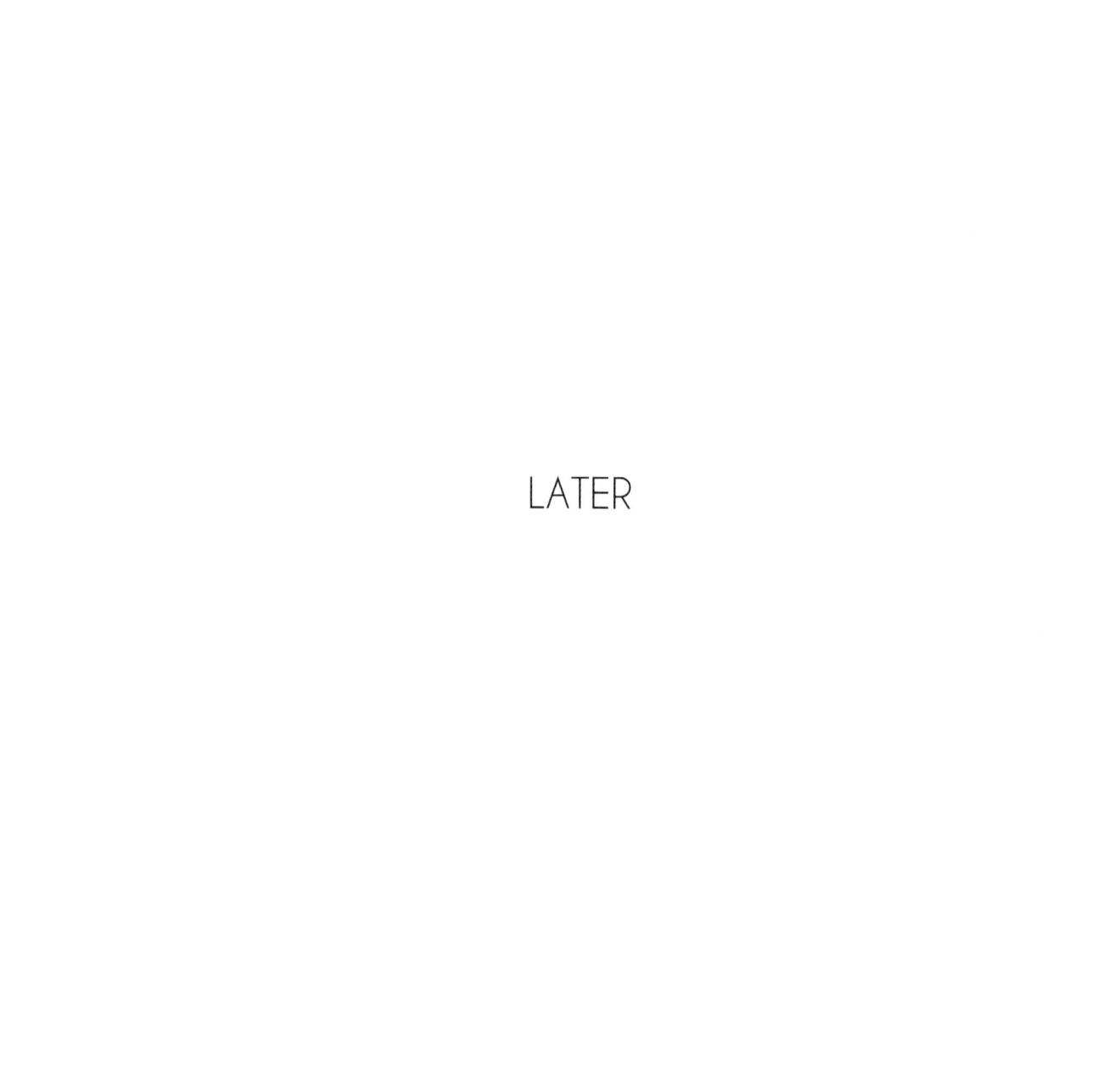

TITLES IN THIS SERIES

Cats of Havana, Cuba
Classic Cars of Havana, Cuba
Gardens of Havana, Cuba
Central Havana, Cuba
Historic Havana, Cuba
The Malecon, Havana, Cuba
Vedado, Havana, Cuba

www.ingramcontent.com/pod-product-compliance
Lightning Source LLC
Chambersburg PA
CBHW051358110526

44592CB00023B/2880